Learning the Language of the Music Business

A Guide to Over 140 Words & Phrases
For Aspiring Music Professionals

Steve Bootland

Index

1 - A&R (ARTIST & REPERTOIRE)

An 'Artist' in the Music Business can be a singer, a guitar player, trumpet player, pianist, drummer or you can even call a whole band "the Artist". 'Repertoire' is like having a collection of trading cards but instead it's a bunch of songs. A&R is like a team of treasure hunters searching the world for hidden music gems, like explorers charting unknown territories in search of buried treasure. They're the magical guides who discover and help new talented artists grow, much like gardeners sniffing out the prettiest flowers, helping them blossom into full bloom. A&R professionals scout for new artists, listen to their music demos, and help shape their direction, like mentors guiding apprentices on a quest for mastery. Just as treasure hunters unearth precious artifacts, A&R professionals unearth musical treasures, bringing them into the light for everyone to admire. A&R is the journey of discovery, where talented people can work together on their dreams coming true.

2 - AIRPLAY

Airplay is like a breeze that carries melodies through the airwaves, like a gentle wind that whispers across the land. It's the enchanting moment when songs take flight and dance on the radio, like colorful birds soaring across the sky. Airplay is when radio stations play music to listeners far and wide, sharing the magic of melodies with eager ears, much like storytellers around a campfire. Airplay fills the airwaves with the sounds of music, creating joy for everyone who listens. Many years ago before people even had TV's the whole family would sit around the radio and listen to their favorite shows. Airplay is the journey that brings music to life, connecting artists' songs with people listening, the audience. If you keep hearing a song you like on the radio, you would be right to say, that song is getting lots of airplay.

3 - ALBUM

An album is like a magical storybook filled with songs instead of words, where each song is like a chapter that takes you on a musical journey, much like the adventures you read about in your favorite books. It's a bit like a box you might keep some of your new favorite toys or games in.

In an album, you can find lots of songs that tell different stories that can give you different feelings, much like the tales you encounter in your favorite stories in books. Whether it's songs about love, friendship, or even fantasy worlds, each song offers a new story that transports you to another place and time. An album could be a bunch of new songs from an artist or even a collection of old songs. There are even albums called "compilation albums" which put together a bunch of songs from different artists like an album with Christmas Songs that has many bands.

Just like how you feel excited and captivated when you dive into a new story or book, listening to an album can give you those same feelings of wonder and excitement as you listen to the melodies and lyrics. An album is like the storybook of music you can enjoy the whole way through.

4 - ARTIST AGENT

An artist agent is like a wise guardian who guides and helps musicians on their journey to play live concerts in front of an audience. Much like a trusted mentor leading a young adventurer through a mysterious forest, they help them navigate this part of the music business like a compass.

In the world of music, artist agents are like knights in shining armor, fighting for the rights of their artists, and defending their kingdom from harm. Artist Agents have the very important job of finding concerts for the artists to play, making sure the artist receives their fair share of the treasures that comes with them.

Similar to how a lighthouse guides ships safely to shore, artist agents illuminate the path to success for musicians, providing help and support every step of the way. An artist agent is more than just a helper, they are a beacon of hope and opportunity, guiding artists towards their dreams of playing in front of people.

5 - ARTIST MANAGER (BAND MANAGER)

An artist manager, also known as a band manager, is like another wise guardian an artist can have by their side. Artist Managers look after the artist or group of musicians, guiding them through their musical journey and protecting them like the Captain of the Ship. It's like having a trusted advisor by your side, helping you navigate the twists and turns of the music industry. A manager takes care of many things so an artist can concentrate on making music. It's a busy job being in a band and there is lots for a manager to do. Managers are defenders of their artists' visions and make sure they receive fair treatment. Just as knights stand by their lords in battle, artist managers stand by their artists, offering support and guidance to help them achieve their musical dreams. So, an artist manager is like the loyal guardian making sure everybody stays on course and reaches their dreams in the world of music.

6 - ASSISTANT ENGINEER

An assistant engineer is like a trusty apprentice in a wizard's workshop, assisting the master in crafting spells and enchantments. They are the Engineer´s right-hand companion, lending a helping hand in the magical process of recording music. In a recording studio, an assistant engineer supports the lead engineer in setting up equipment, and ensuring the smooth operation of the recording session, like a devoted apprentice following their mentor's lead with dedication and excitement. Just as apprentices learn from their masters to become skilled craftsmen, assistant engineers learn from experienced audio engineers to become good in their craft.

7 - AUDIO

Audio is all the sounds you hear when listening to music, watching TV or even playing a video game, like a messenger that carries sounds through the air. A bird singing its sweet melody in the early morning is audio. It's the invisible force that brings music, voices, and sound effects to our ears, like a gentle whisper that tickles our senses. Without audio, there would be no sound.

In the world of technology, audio is like a powerful tool that allows us to capture and share sounds with others, whether it's music, speech, or noise far away. It is how we experience the world around us with hearing, like a window opening onto a vast landscape of sonic wonders.

<h1 style="text-align:center">8 - AUDITION</h1>

An audition is where performers showcase their talents in front of others, like having to pick one friend to be in your play. It's a process where artists present their music in front of directors, producers, or judges, with a golden opportunity to shine and sparkle. Just like TV talent shows, sometimes they can be good and everyone likes the music, and sometimes they don´t go very well. Don´t worry though, you can't please everyone all the time. There is always a next time to try again.

In the world of music and bands, auditions are like enchanted gates that open doors to new opportunities and adventures. They're moments of excitement and anticipation, resembling a thrilling ride on a magical carousel where dreams take flight. If you want to play in a football team, sometimes you have to try out. A band might be looking for a guitar player and people could audition to join and hope to get picked. An audition could even be for an orchestra.

<h1 style="text-align:center">9 - BACKGROUND MUSIC</h1>

Background music plays softly around you, setting the mood for whatever you're doing. Much like a gentle breeze that whispers through the trees on a sunny day. When you watch a movie, sometimes the music you hear can help make you laugh or even make you scared.

Background music can be found all around us; in cafes and restaurants to shopping malls and elevators. Sometimes it can even change your mood, much like the soft glow of fireflies lighting up the night sky can make you happy. Background Music could be soothing melodies that help you relax or upbeat tunes that energize and inspire you, making even the simplest moments feel special.

Background music has the power to lift your spirits and transport you to different worlds, turning ordinary moments into exciting ones. Background music is like the magical melody that weaves its way through your life, adding color and harmony to every moment, whether you're playing, studying, or simply enjoying the beauty of the world around you.

<h1 style="text-align:center">10 - BACKING VOCALIST</h1>

A backing vocalist is like an echo that adds enchantment to a song, like the wind through trees. Imagine you are a singer and a friend sings parts of a song with you to make it sound better, like birds singing in harmony on a sunny morning. A backing vocalist sings some parts with the lead singer, adding harmonies, lifting the performance with their magical vocal talent. It might even be another member of the band who has a good singing voice that fits well. Just as friends join hands to dance in circles, backing vocalists join voices to create a blend that delights listeners. A backing vocalist is like the companion who supports the lead singer and adds their own magic to the song with their voice.

11 - BACKLINE TECHNICIAN

A backline technician is like a master craftsman behind the scenes, ensuring that every instrument on stage is finely tuned and ready to unleash its musical magic. Backline is a word that describes all the equipment and instruments musicians use. They're like the secret keepers of the band's arsenal or a mechanic for instruments, setting up the equipment that brings the music to life and keeping them all in great shape. Backline technicians work very hard to ensure that guitars are perfectly tuned, drums are finely tuned, and keyboards are in perfect working order, like the caretakers of a musical workshop. Sometimes you might hear the word 'Roadie' which can describe a lot of people that help behind the stage. Backline Technicians sometimes have their own special skills they are good at, like fixing guitars or keyboards. A backline technician is like the unsung hero who ensures that the musical machinery runs smoothly, allowing the band to shine on stage.

12 - BASSIST

A bassist is like the sturdy foundation of a castle and part of the heartbeat of a band. They play a big guitar called a bass guitar which usually has 4 strings and sometimes 6 strings. Bass guitars make a deep low sound that you can feel in your chest and help keep the

beat of the music. Bassists hold a solid groove with powerful notes helping other instruments shine out and stay in time together. Bassists are like the secret sauce that adds the flavor to the music.

13 - BLANKET LICENSE

A Blanket License isn't a special license that lets you carry a blanket around, which could also be fun to have. A blanket license is like a golden ticket that gives businesses permission to play many different songs. Imagine you had a special ticket that let you go see as many movies as you want to in a whole year?. It's a special agreement that allows businesses to play music from a big list without every band or artist giving permission to say it's ok. It's like having access to a treasure trove of melodies and rhythms.

In the world of music, a blanket license is like a tool that lets restaurants, stores, or even hotels play lots of different songs to their customers. Similar to how a shield protects a knight from harm in battle, a blanket license shields businesses from playing music in public without permission which they must have. The businesses pay some money for this license and the people who made the songs get paid some of that money for their hard work.

14 - BOOKER

A booker is like the organizer of a big party helping musicians spread their music far and wide. They are scouts seeking out artists and making pathways for them to play their music. Bookers help find the artists and bands to play at shows, parties, festivals and events. Next time you see your favorite band playing you can thank a booker for helping them get there.

15 - BUSKING

When you see musicians playing songs outside in places like train stations, subways or public squares, they´re called 'Buskers'. Buskers can be musicians, magicians, jugglers, dancers or even human statues standing perfectly still. For musicians, busking is a great way to practice playing music to people in public and fun as well. You can play other artists' songs or even some of your own songs just to see if people like them. It's a good way to practice your new songs too. Next time you see a street performer busking, stop and give them a listen, you may be surprised. There are many great buskers out there on the street.

A cassette is like a magical scroll filled with enchanting melodies, where music is stored and played back with a simple press of a button. Back in the old days before CD´s and streaming like Spotify, people listened to music from cassettes in machines called Cassette Decks which could play the special tape that the music was stored on. There was a side A and a side B, both with some songs to play. Cassettes can be fun to collect and many bands still have their music on them for fans to buy. A cassette is more than just a piece of plastic and tape, it's like a timeless artifact in the ever-changing world of music. For fun, ask your grandparents how they used to rewind cassettes back to the beginning. They will probably tell you a long story about twirling it on the end of a pencil to help save more time the batteries might last for.

17 - CATALOG

A catalog is like a library full of all your favorite stories or games. For music, it's a treasure trove where you can find a collection of songs and albums, just like how you might find a big selection of books or games at your favorite store. It is a list of all the songs a musician, a record label or a music publisher has to offer. When a musician talks about their catalog, they are talking about all of the songs they have made.

In a big music catalog, you might discover all sorts of songs from different artists and genres, much like exploring different sections of a library or in a game store to find something new and exciting to enjoy. Like a book shelf, you can arrange your catalog in a tidy way so it is easy to find the song you are looking for. Whether you like pop music, rock, hip-hop, or something else, there's something for everyone in big music catalogs.

18 - CMO (Collective Management Organization)

A CMO, or Collective Management Organization, is like a team of superheroes, each with their own special powers. CMOs collect money, called royalties, from various places just like the King's Royal Tax Collectors. They receive royalties from places like radio stations, streaming services, and for live performances, making sure that artists receive fair payment for their work when their song has been played. Artists can sign up with a CMO very easily once they start to record music. Just as knights gather in guilds to protect their kingdom, musicians rely on CMOs to protect their rights and ensure they receive their rightful share of the rewards. A CMO acts as the guardian of creative treasures, ensuring that the magic of music continues.

19 - COLLABORATION (COLLAB)

Collaboration, or "collab" for short, is where two or more artists come together, blending their talents and creativity to make music together. It's when individuals work together towards an epic quest. Like when you invite friends over to help build the coolest Lego castle and it looks great.

In the world of music, collaboration is like a recipe where each ingredient adds its own flavor to the mix. Artists collaborate on songs, performances, and projects, forming a colorful mosaic where their own talents come together to create something beautiful. Sometimes two heads are better than one if you have an idea of a song and want to work on it with somebody else.

20 - COMPOSITION

Composition is the process of writing and arranging music like a magician's wand weaving musical notes together. Or like painting a picture with sounds, using instruments as brushes to bring your musical painting to life. All the bits of the song, like notes and melodies all together are called the composition. Whether you are writing a catchy pop song, a dance hit or even a grand symphony, the Composition is the special ingredients of notes, chords and rhythms that a chef would use to create a musical dish.

21 - COVER SONG

A cover song is like trying to make your favorite recipe, where you add their own special ingredients to create a fresh and exciting version of a tasty dish from a different chef. It's also like a costume party where each person dresses up as their favorite character, adding their own style. A cover song is when one artist performs a song which was written and recorded by another artist, mixing it with their own style. A bit like putting a new twist on a classic tale. There are bands that only play other peoples songs called 'cover bands'. Just as friends share stories and memories at a party, musicians share their love for music through cover songs, sometimes playing songs from their favorite musical heroes. So, a cover song is like the musical potluck where artists bring their own flavor to the table.

22 - COWBELL

A cowbell is like a cheerful companion in the rhythm section, its bright clangy sound can sometimes add a touch of joy to the music, much like a playful jingle of bells on a winter's day. A Cowbell is a percussion instrument that looks like a big metal bell you might see on a cow in a field.

In the world of percussion, the cowbell adds mood to the groove. It's an instrument used in many types of music, from rock and pop to Latin and jazz, resembling a colorful gem in the treasure chest of percussion sounds.

Similar to how laughter brings warmth to a room, the sound of a cowbell lifts spirits and invites listeners to join in the rhythm. The cowbell is more than just a simple instrument. It's also fun in the music business to say, everything needs more cowbell. Like, "school was fun today but it could have used more cowbell."

23 - CUE SHEET

Imagine you are watching a movie and the hero is about to save the day. A cue sheet is like a special map that tells all the people making the movie when they should start playing part of a song they want to use, and when to finish playing it. When a film is made, they usually put the music in after it's all filmed on camera. Cue sheets are an important tool for showing everybody when to play the song, the name of the song and even the name of the artist who wrote the song. Just as sailors rely on maps to navigate through uncharted waters, music supervisors can even use cue sheets to pay royalties to the right artist. A cue sheet is like the guide that illuminates the path for music to fit exactly where they want it to play in a movie or on TV.

24 - CURFEW

A curfew is a time when a concert needs to finish. It's like a rule made by grown-ups to help keep children and families safe, like a friendly reminder to return home before the stars come out.

Just as how parents tuck their children into bed at night, a concert may have a curfew telling the band what time all the loud noise must finish. Sometimes that is very late and sometimes it is early so everyone can get home safe. If a concert is really big and loud there might be a curfew of 9 o´clock or later so the neighborhood can get some rest.

25 - C WITH A CIRCLE AROUND IT (©)

The "C with a circle around it" is like a special shield that protects a musician's or songwriter's work. It's like putting your name on a drawing you made, but instead of just your name, it's a special symbol that means 'Copyright' and says, "This music belongs to me." When you see the "C with a circle around it," it means that someone created that music, and they have special rights to decide how it's used and who can use it. So, it's like a special seal that helps musicians keep their music safe and makes sure they get the credit for writing it and even get paid some of the money they deserve.

26 - DAW (DIGITAL AUDIO WORKSTATION)

A DAW, short for Digital Audio Workstation, is like a workshop where music creators craft their songs, much like a laboratory where inventors create amazing gadgets. It's a treasure chest of electronic tools and gadgets that help musicians bring their music to life, whether they're recording their voice, playing instruments, or adding special effects like reverb or echo with this very helpful software.

In a DAW, you can mix and edit sounds just like a painter mixes colors on their palette, allowing you to create music that's as unique as you are. Just as magicians use tools to perform their tricks, musicians use a DAW to craft sounds that captivate listeners and transport them to new places. So, a DAW is like a workshop where you can unleash your creativity and bring your musical dreams to life, whether it's music for battling dragons, dancing with bears, or soaring through the stars.

A decibel measures how loud or quiet sounds are when you turn a volume knob up or down. Even the noises coming from outside can be measured in decibels (dB).

In the world of sound, a decibel is a unit of measurement like when you use a thermometer to take your temperature. A Decibel tells us the intensity or level of sound, like how bright a star shines in the night sky. It helps us understand whether a noise is gentle like the rustle of leaves or powerful like the roar of a lion.

Just as how a wizard needs to control their magic to avoid causing chaos, understanding decibels helps us manage sound to protect our ears and enjoy the world around us safely. A whisper might be 30 decibels while talking with your friends outside might be 60 decibels. A loud motorcycle speeding by might be 90 decibels or more. So, a decibel is like a ruler that helps us measure the volume of the symphony of sounds that surrounds us every day!

28 - DEMO

A demo is like a sneak peek or a special preview of something exciting, much like a teaser trailer for a new movie coming or a demo version of a video game that lets you try it out before it's finished.

In the music world, a demo is a rough recording of a song or piece of music, created to give listeners a taste of what's to come, like a preview of the full adventure. It might not be perfect, but it's like a rough sketch that lets you imagine how amazing the final version will be.

Just like how you feel excited and curious when you see a sneak peek of your favorite movie or game, listening to a demo can excite you as you imagine the finished masterpiece. A demo gives you a glimpse into the enchanting world of music, sparking your imagination and leaving you eager for more.

29 - DERIVATIVE WORK

A derivative work is like a potion brewed from your favorite story, adding new ingredients to create an exciting adventure, much like a delicious new recipe that puts a twist on an old favorite dish. It's like playing a game where you take a familiar character and story and imagine new adventures for them, like dressing up dolls in different outfits to create unique looks.

In music, a derivative work is when a musician takes a song or piece of music that someone else already made and changes it a lot adding their own special touch to it, like mixing in new beats or writing new lyrics. It's like taking a fairy tale and giving it a modern twist, making it fresh and exciting for a new generation of listeners. It's different from making a cover song because a cover song copies the original song and a derivative work changes the original song more.

Just as artists use their imagination to create new worlds in stories and games, musicians use their creativity to transform existing music into something new and unique. However, it's important to remember that anyone who creates a derivative work using someone else's song should ask the original artist or an adult in the music business if they have permission to change their song.

30 - DIGITAL DISTRIBUTION

Digital distribution is like a magical messenger owl that can deliver a message to all of your friends around the world in the blink of an eye. A network of pathways that carry music from the creators to listeners everywhere through the internet. It's like a vast web of connected portals, allowing musicians to share their songs with audiences far and wide. With digital distribution, artists can get their music to online platforms like streaming services and music stores, making it instantly accessible to fans on their computers and phones with just a few clicks. It's like opening a gateway to a global audience, where music can travel across borders and cultures easily. When you look at an artist on Spotify you can read a little bit about them when you click on "About". There you can see a few of the popular cities and countries that really like their music. Digital distribution helps artists reach listeners in every corner of the globe, breaking down barriers and spreading the magic of music far and wide.

31 - DIGITAL RELEASE

A digital release is like sending out magical messages to share music with people all over the world through the internet. It's like waving a wand and instantly making your music available for anyone to listen to, wherever they are. Instead of waiting for CDs or records to be made, artists can upload their songs to platforms like Spotify, Apple Music, or Youtube, where fans can discover and enjoy them with just a few clicks. If an artist has a new song or album on CD, that would be called a physical release. A digital release allows music to travel through cyberspace and reach listeners in every corner of the globe through computers, ipads or even your phone.

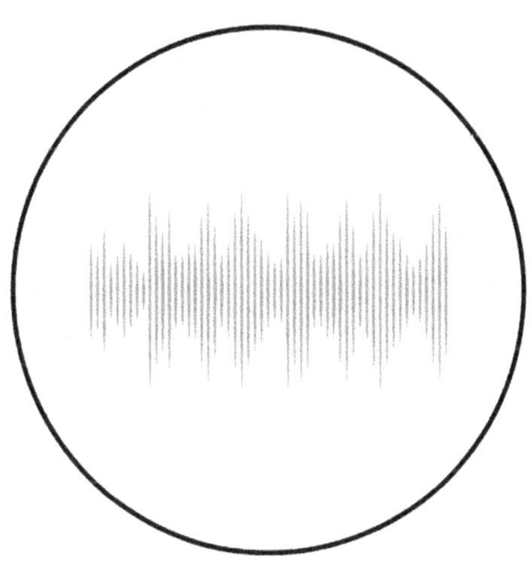

32 - DIGITAL SERVICE PROVIDER (DSP)

A Digital Service Provider, or DSP, is like a gateway to lots and lots of melodies and rhythms. It is where Digital Releases shine out. DSP´s like Spotify, Apple Music and Youtube bring music from all around the world right to your fingertips, no matter where you are.

A DSP is a platform, like an app or website, where you can listen to and discover music online, much like a library where you can explore endless shelves of songs and albums. It is where your digital release will live. Whether you're in the mood for pop, rock, jazz, or anything else, a DSP has a wide variety of music to suit your tastes.

Just like how you can explore new worlds and adventures in your favorite books or games, a DSP lets you explore new artists and songs with just a few clicks.

33 - DIRECT TO FAN

Direct to fan is a great way artists can get their music to their followers. It is like a special pathway that connects musicians directly with their most devoted fans, much like a secret club where friends gather to laugh and play. It's like a bridge that allows artists to meet with fans, and maybe even offer them special merchandise you can´t find in stores. Direct to fan platforms let musicians build relationships with their fans, offering them new experiences and personal interactions, like having a special party for your closest friends. Just as friends exchange letters and gifts to show their appreciation, musicians use direct to fan channels to say thanks to their fans and reward their loyalty with special treats and surprises. Direct to fan is like a path that brings artists and fans together in a community, making connections and spreading joy through the power of music.

34 - DOUBLEDRIVE

Doubledrive is like having two supercharged engines powering a rocket ship. In music, it refers to a technique where a guitarist plays two notes at the same time, creating a powerful and energetic sound. It's like when you're riding a bike and pedal with both your feet as fast as you can, zooming down the road with double the speed and excitement. Doubledrive adds an extra punch to the music, like a superhero unleashing their full strength to save the day. So, it's like doubling the fun and intensity to rock the stage with electrifying energy! A band's tour bus driver might also use the word doubledrive. That is when the next concert can be so far away that they might need two drivers to take turns so they don't get too tired.

35 - DRUMMER

A drummer is the heartbeat of a band, setting the rhythm and pulse that brings music to life, much like the steady throb of a dragon's wings as it soars through the sky. A commander of an enchanted army, leading the charge with thunderous beats, like a valiant knight rallying their troops for battle. A drummer keeps the band in sync like a ticking clock, driving the energy forward and adding excitement to the musical journey. A drummer is like the magical force that propels music forward, giving it energy and making sure that listeners are swept away on a thrilling adventure with every beat.

36 - EFFECTS PEDALS

Effects pedals are like magic buttons for guitar players. When a musician steps on them, they make cool sounds, like making your voice super deep or turning it into a robot voice. It's like having special powers to change how your guitar sounds, just like how you can change your voice when you pretend to be different characters. There are many types of effects pedals that can change the sound by adding effects. Some have funny names like RAT or BOSS and Big Muff, Wah Wah and Fuzz Pedals.

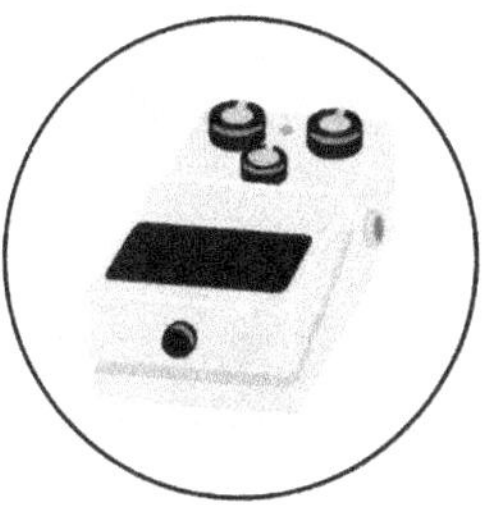

37 - ELECTRONIC MUSIC

Electronic music is like a sonic playground where sounds are crafted using technology and imagination, not using instruments like guitars or piano.. It's a genre of music where musicians use electronic devices and computers to create fun new sounds, like a futuristic laboratory where experiments in sound take place.
In the world of music, electronic music has many styles, from pulsating electronic dance music beats to quiet relaxing music that lets you relax or "Chill". Pretend you have a canvas where you can paint with sound. With electronic music you can paint whatever you like.

Similar to how explorers chart new territories, electronic musicians can always venture into uncharted sonic lands in sound.

38 - EPK (Electronic Press Kit)

An EPK is like a musician´s own story book on their computer which they send to people who need to know more about them. It's a portal that transports journalists, promoters, and music industry people into the heart of an artist's creative universe. An EPK has information about a musician, like their biography, photos, videos, music, and concert tour dates, serving as a guide to their artistic journey. Music Industry people use EPKs to explore the musical landscape and discover new talents waiting to be uncovered. An EPK is like the enchanted gateway that invites the world to step in and learn more about the artist.

39 - FLIGHTCASE

A flightcase is like a Pirate chest that protects precious treasures, much like a sturdy fortress guards against invaders. It's a special container made of strong materials, such as wood or metal, made to keep valuable items safe during travel.

In the world of music, a flightcase is used to transport delicate equipment, like musical instruments or sound gear, from one place to another. Much like a spaceship carries astronauts through the vastness of space, It's like having a protective shield around your belongings, ensuring they arrive at their destination unharmed and ready for action. Kind of like a suitcase that is super hard to damage.

Just as knights wear suits of armor to defend themselves in battle, musicians rely on flightcases to shield their gear from bumps, knicks, and rough handling during journeys. They are like guardians that keep your musical treasures safe and sound, whether you're traveling to distant lands or even playing close to home.

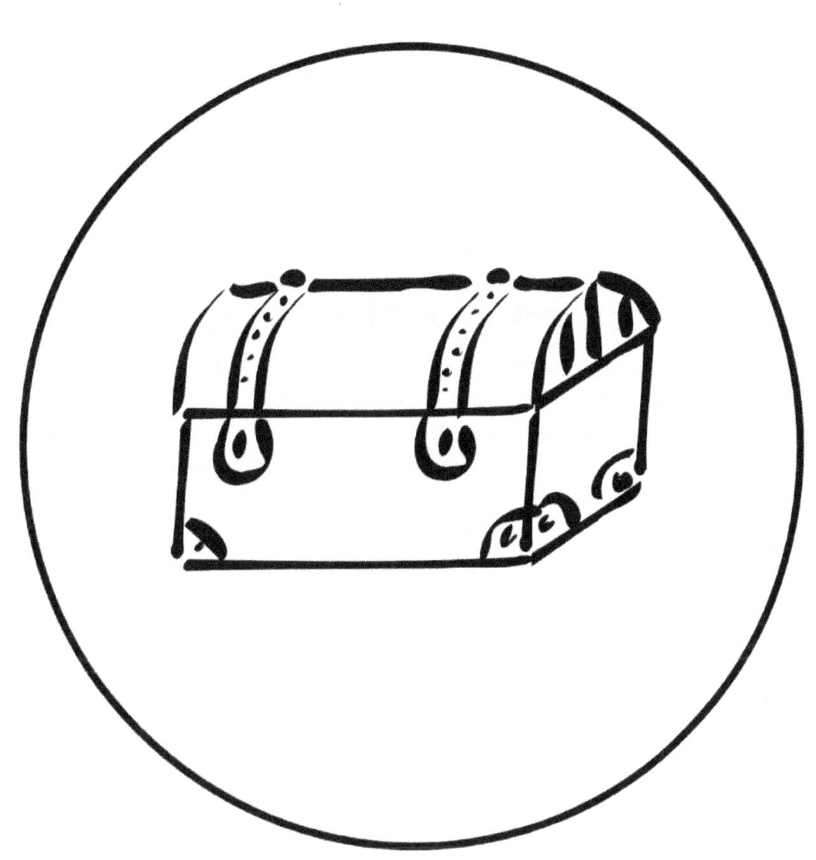

40 - FLOOR TOM

A floor tom is a big drum that sits low to the ground, adding deep and powerful beats to the music. It's like the booming footsteps of a great Giant walking through the forest, making the ground shake with each step. In a drum kit, the floor tom is like the mighty warrior in an army of drums, providing a solid foundation for the rhythm. When played, it's like unleashing a thunderstorm of sound, adding excitement to the music. So, the floor tom is like the mighty drum that commands attention and drives the beat forward with its powerful presence.

41 - FOH

FOH stands for Front of House. It's like the special area in a concert where all the sound and light magic happens for the audience. It's where the sound engineer and lighting director sits, making sure everything sounds perfect for everyone listening. Imagine it's like the control center of a spaceship, where the captain (the sound engineer and lighting director) steers the ship (the music) through the galaxy (the concert venue), ensuring a smooth and fun journey for everyone onboard (the audience). So, FOH is like the command center where the magic of sound and lights comes to life for everyone to enjoy.

42 - FOLLOWERS

Followers are like friends or fans who enjoy keeping up with what you're doing, kind of like the people who follow their favorite gamers or artists on social media. They're like a supportive group of buddies who cheer you on and enjoy seeing every new thing you do.

When you post something cool or share your thoughts online, your followers see it and can like it, comment, or share it with others, much like how you and your friends play and talk about stuff you like to do. They're like a virtual squad who enjoys hanging out with you online and sharing in your interests and adventures. Sometimes musicians with lots of followers attract more fans to their music who just want to see why so many people are following them. Like a snowball rolling down the hill gets bigger and bigger. The more followers musicians have means more people will get to hear new songs they write when they put them on Digital Service Providers.

Having followers online can make you feel connected to others who enjoy what you do! So, followers are like an awesome group of buddies who support you and make you feel special, whether you're sharing music, games, or just fun moments from your day.

43 - FX RACK

An FX rack is like a toolbox filled with exciting tools that add special effects and textures to the sound of instruments and voices. With lots of buttons and flashing lights FX Racks are ready to help the sonic sound of a concert performance or recording. An FX rack has a collection of electronic devices called "effects processors". They have names which sometimes sound like the job they are supposed to do such as reverb, delay, and distortion units, each with its own unique way to change the sound. Just as alchemists blend ingredients to create potions, sound engineers use processors in the FX rack to craft the perfect sound potion. An FX rack is like the sorcerer's arsenal, empowering sound wizards to weave spells of sonic enchantment and create fun musical experiences.

44 - GAMING MUSIC COMPOSER

A gaming music composer crafts enchanting melodies and thrilling music for the adventures you have when you play video games, much like a storyteller weaving magical tales for you to explore. Music and sound can make your game even more awesome.

A gaming music composer creates music for games, whether it's epic battle themes to pump up your excitement or quiet or soft melodies to soothe your soul during quiet moments, much like a tailor sewing a custom-made cloak to fit the hero of the story. Their music helps set the tone, create tension, and create emotions, making your gaming experience even more fun. Some song writers only like making music especially for games so they are called Gaming Music Composers.

The music created by a gaming music composer can make you feel like you're part of the action. So, a gaming music composer is like the magical maestro behind the scenes, orchestrating the symphony of sounds that brings your favorite games to life, making every quest and battle an unforgettable adventure.

45 - GRANT WRITERS

Imagine if a musician or band is invited to play concerts in another country but they haven't saved up enough money to get there. Or imagine if you have your own idea to make a big concert and you plan to give all the money you make to a very special cause. Things like these can cost more money than you have, but sometimes there are places you can go to get help. Some governments and organizations offer 'grants' which is some money to help you if they think you deserve to have it. Other people might want to ask for a grant at the same time, and they may not have many grants to give so they only pick the best projects. You have to have a very good reason why you want the money.

Grant writers help you paint a picture with words to show why it should be your project that gets the grant (money). Grant writers are really good at painting a picture using words. Like storytellers they weave together everything needed to make your project sound great.

46 - GUITAR RIFF

A guitar riff is like a catchy bit of musical notes played on the guitar that grabs listeners attention, drawing them into the rhythm and groove of the song. It's like a musical magnet that grabs your attention and sticks in your mind long after the music fades away. It's part of the guitar notes in a song that hooks you. You might even catch yourself humming the riff for no reason from time to time. These catchy riffs are hard not to hum along to, like part of a favorite song that stays with you throughout the day. Just as skilled painters craft masterpieces with their hands, guitarists craft riffs that elevate songs to new heights, creating musical moments you remember.

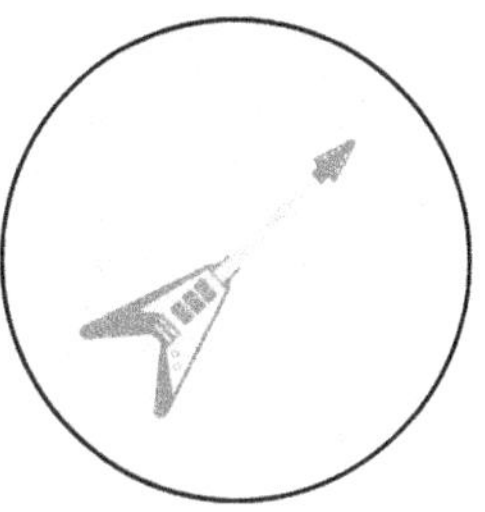

47 - HEADLINER

A headliner is much like the hero of an epic tale who leads the adventure. They're the main attraction of a concert, the musician or band that everyone has been eagerly waiting to see and the last ones to play at a concert when more than one band is playing. They are usually the ones you really wanted to see the most.

In the world of concerts, a headliner is the main act that wields their musical talents to enchant the audience and create unforgettable moments. They can be like a beacon that lights up the night sky, making every concert an experience filled with excitement!

48 - HI HATS

Hi-hats are little cymbals that make music sparkle and shimmer. They're a pair of shiny metal discs that sit on a stand and are played with the drummer's foot on a pedal, creating a crisp and rhythmic sound. Imagine they're like a bird´s wings fluttering in the air, adding a sprinkle of magic to the music. In a drum kit, the hi-hats help keep the beat and add texture to the sound, like the steady tick-tock of a clock. Hi-hats are like a secret ingredient that gives music its special sparkle and groove.

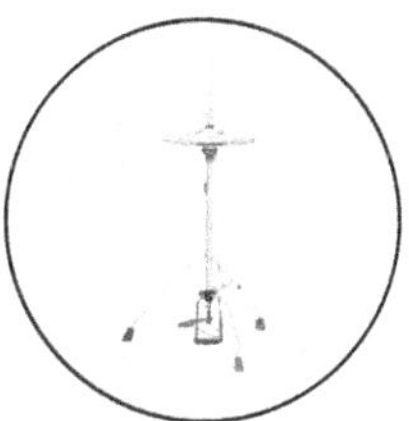

49 - HOOK

A hook is like a musical magnet, drawing listeners in with its catchy tune and keeping their
excitement throughout the song, much like a captivating story that holds your attention from
beginning to end. Remember we said a guitar riff could hook you?. A hook is a very catchy part
of a song that hooks you in. Sometimes it is a bit in a song where it changes a little and makes
you sit up. Maybe you didn't expect it to change but like it very much. It can be a fun part of a
song that everyone remembers or it can be a dramatic scary bit even.
In the world of music, a hook leads listeners through the song's twists and turns which you will
remember easily, much like the best part of a delicious meal that leaves you craving more. A
hook is the heart and soul of a song, which you may by humming for long after.

50 - HORNS

Horns are like majestic heralds announcing the arrival of the king, much like royal trumpeters
heralding the dawn of a new era. They are shiny instruments made from brass and can be
trumpets, trombones, tubas, French Horns and more. Even a Saxophone can be in the horn
section of a band. Horn Sections are usually found in orchestras, jazz bands, marching bands,
pop bands and sound like bold strokes of color on a canvas of sound.

Similar to how a conductor leads an orchestra with sweeping gestures, horn players command
their instruments with skill. Horns are part of a group called wind instruments because you have
to use your breath to blow in them like the wind.

51 - INDEPENDENT LABEL

Imagine you want to make music for everyone to hear but you don't want to have lots of other people making all the important decisions for you. Pretend you have a small cottage away from a big Kingdom. You and friends make songs together in the cottage without some of the rules of the big bustling kingdom nearby. It makes you feel more comfortable working in the cottage with less people. In the Kingdom there might be big record label companies that can help you get your music to your fans but maybe you like making music at your cottage hidden in the enchanted forest. That is a bit like an independent label, where artists can find refuge and a bit more freedom than some of the major record labels in the big kingdom. Some musicians like to work with independent labels because they feel it´s more like a club where they can be more free, without the bustle and all your friends are members. Both independent and major labels can be good places for musicians to go if they don't want to do everything on their own to get their music to fans. Working with a good team of people you like is important.

Whether you are a singer with a heart full of songs or a band with dreams as big as the sky, sometimes an independent record label can feel like a special place where your music can fly free.

52 - IN EAR MONITORS

Sometimes an excited crowd at a concert can be very noisy and drums and guitars can be loud too. Music can be a noisy business. Have you ever watched a singer and it looked like they were listening to ipods when they were singing with something in their ears?. In-ear monitors are like high-tech earpieces that bring the music the whole band is playing directly to the ears of the performer. The Sound Engineer or a special technician called a 'Monitor Engineer' sends a mix of the music the whole band is playing to the performer when they are playing so they can stay in tune and stay in sync with the rest of the band. In-ear monitors are like sophisticated tools that help the musical experience for musicians, so they can perform at their best. In their ears they can hear their own voices while singing so they can tell if they are singing ok. If they are playing an instrument, they can hear that as well. That way they can walk around the stage and closer to the loud audience but they will still be able to hear themselves.

53 - IN-FLIGHT MUSIC

In-flight music is like a comforting companion that travels with you on your journey through the skies, like a friendly cloud drifting alongside your airplane. It's the soundtrack to your flying adventure, setting the mood and easing your mind during the flight, similar to a gentle breeze that soothes your soul. Listening to music on the in-flight entertainment system on airplanes is fun, just like watching the movies or playing the games they might have on the plane.

In-flight music helps passengers get through the ups and downs of air travel, offering moments of joy or to help relax them. It can feel like a very long trip if you don't have some music to listen to. In-flight music is also a great way for musicians to get their music to people that have never heard of them before. When you have nothing to do for hours on a plane, it can be fun to listen to bands and songs you don't know yet. Maybe you will discover your new favorite band or song on your next plane trip.

54 - IN PERPETUITY

"In perpetuity" is like a spell that lasts forever, like a never-ending story or an eternal flame that never goes out. When something is "in perpetuity," it means it will continue forever without coming to an end. It's like planting a seed that grows into a timeless tree, standing tall and strong for many years to come. Granting something "in perpetuity" can sometimes help protect it from ever being lost or forgotten. Whenever you see "In Perpetuity" in music, you must decide if it is good for you to do that though. If you let a friend borrow a toy, you might hope they give it back some time because you don't really want to give it to them forever. Letting someone use your music "In Perpetuity" could mean that they never have to give your song back to you and they can decide how the song is used. You may not want that; maybe it's ok for them to use your song for a little while but not forever. When you see "In Perpetuity" it's usually a good idea to ask a music lawyer to help you decide if it's good for you to agree to it.

An input list is like a recipe that helps the sound engineer know which instruments and voices are going to be part of a performance or recording. It's like writing down the ingredients you need to make your favorite potion or spell. In the world of a sound engineer, an input list tells them what equipment and microphones they'll need to set up for each part of the music. Every microphone will have its own number or 'channel' on the input list and the same number on the mixing desk. Just like following a recipe step by step to create a delicious meal, the input list guides the engineers in preparing the stage or studio to capture the magic of the music. On the input list it might say channel number 1 is the singer's voice. Channel 2 might say it is the singer's guitar. The engineer would plug in the singer's microphone to channel 1 and the guitar to channel 2. When they follow the input list they know where all the instruments are on the mixing desk and they can adjust each one and mix all the music together. So, an input list is like the map that makes sure everything gets plugged in to the right place in a recording studio or at a live concert.

56 - INSTRUMENTAL

Instrumental music is like a painting without words, where melodies and rhythms speak volumes without saying a single thing, much like a silent movie that tells a story without sound. An instrumental is a song without words or "lyrics".

In the world of music, instrumentals offer a blank canvas for listeners' imaginations to roam free, much like an open field where anything is possible. Without lyrics to guide the listener, instrumental music allows them to imagine a story in their own way. Sometimes a song can have lyrics that an engineer or producer can simply take away leaving just the music. This is called the "Instrumental version" of your song. A Sound Engineer can do that very easily by just cutting out the channel that says "Vocals". That way you can offer fans a song with words (lyrics) and an instrumental version they can play. Have you ever sang karaoke or played games where you sing along to a song you know with a microphone? Those games are playing the instrumental version of the song so other people can sing the lyrics. TV commercials sometimes play instrumental versions of songs while someone else is talking.

57 - JINGLE

A jingle is like a catchy melody that dances into your ears and stays in your head, much like a playful tune that whispers secrets of joy and delight. It is usually a short bit of music, made especially for a product, brand, TV Advert or idea. A jingle should feel like a gateway to a world of imagination where dreams come true and anything is possible. A Jingle for a restaurant might be really short and doesn´t have any words but when you hear it, you remember the food and want to go there. If it's your favorite restaurant, a good jingle might make you hungry whenever you hear a little bit of the music which reminds you about it.

58 - KEYBOARDS

Keyboards are electronic instruments that produce many different sounds, from soft melodies to powerful bass sounds, much like a big toolbox offering various tools for different tasks. They're musical devices with keys like a piano that you press to generate music.

In music, keyboards allow musicians to create lots of different sounds, whether it's the roar of a lion or the gentle rustle of leaves. They offer many tones and effects at your fingertips, like a treasure trove of sonic options waiting to be explored.

Similar to how a painter mixes colors to create a masterpiece, musicians use keyboards to blend sounds and craft harmonies that listeners may like. A keyboard might have 100 different piano sounds too.

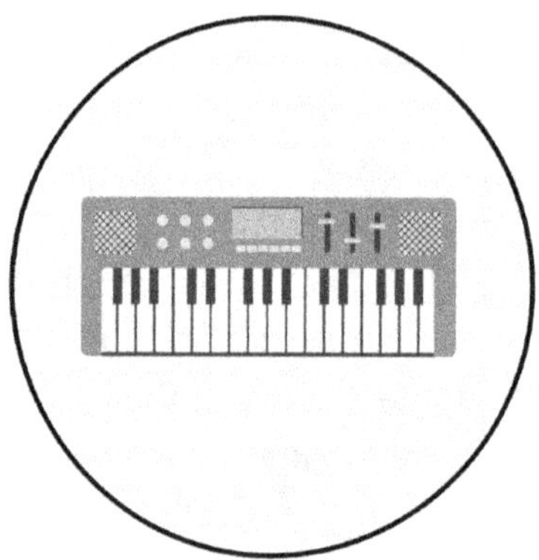

59 - LICENSE AGREEMENT

A license agreement is a contract between you and somebody else, much like a promise made between friends to share their toys and games. It's a special agreement that tells you the rules for using something valuable that someone else created, like music, software, or artwork.

In a license agreement, one person gives permission to another to use their creation in special ways, like how a king might grant permission for knights to use his land for farming, with rules to make sure everyone knows what they can and cannot do on the land. Especially when they must give the land back to the King. In music you can license your songs to a record label for an amount of time and when the time is up all your music gets returned to you. Remember we talked about "in Perpetuity" which means forever? A licensing agreement is a good way to be able to get all your songs back after a short amount of time that you agree on. When someone licenses songs from you, they must pay you something too, like sharing any extra treasure they can get while they have it.

60 - LIGHTING DIRECTOR

A lighting director is the maestro of illumination, orchestrating the visual magic of a live performance. They're like the painters of light, using beams and colors to create wonderful landscapes on stage. A lighting director works closely with the music, creating a mood with rhythm and lighting effects. It's like conducting a symphony of lights which look great when you are watching a band play. Just as artists use brushes to create masterpieces on canvas, lighting directors use their expertise to paint scenes of enchantment with light. While you listen to the music the lighting director transforms the stage with a magical dance of light, colors and shadows.

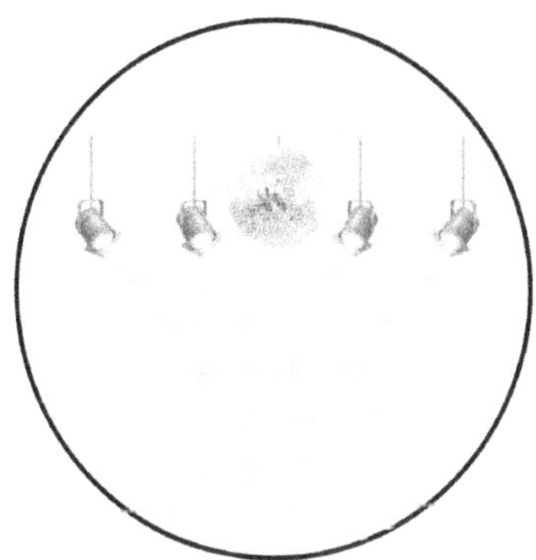

61 - LYRICS

Lyrics are the words to a song. They are the part of the music that you sing along to, like the lines of your favorite movie or words in a story book. Just like how stories have characters and plots, songs have lyrics that can tell a story with feelings and emotions. The Lyrics can make you happy, or even sad. Next time you are humming along to a tune, pay attention to the lyrics - they might just speak to you in a special way. It can be fun to take your lyrics and have them translated into a different language than yours too. That way other countries get to know about your music and you can make more friends and fans there.

62 - LYRICIST

A lyricist is like a masterful storyteller, skillfully crafting tales and feelings into songs, much like a gifted narrator spinning engaging stories around a campfire. They're like a poet of melodies, able to paint pictures with words and tunes, similar to an artist creating beautiful images with their brush.

A lyricist writes the words, or 'lyrics', to songs, expressing feelings, stories, and messages that touch listeners' hearts, similar to a wise person sharing knowledge with their stories. Just as a painter uses colors to convey emotions a lyricist uses words to create images and feelings, taking listeners on a journey through the magic of music. Some musicians might like to write the lyrics more than they like playing an instrument. Some people are great storytellers.

Whether singing about love, friendship, or even imaginary new worlds, lyricists have the power to create laughter, tears, and dreams through their lyrics. Some of the money made from royalties of a song can come from lyrics. In fact there are more ways lyrics can really help. Lyrics can be translated into languages from other countries. Imagine how many more fans you could make around the world if they could all understand your lyrics. You could even print some of your lyrics on T-Shirts for fans to buy. A lyricist is the skilled storyteller who breathes life into words through music, leaving a lasting impact on those who listen.

63 - MASTERING

Mastering is like the final touch-up before sharing a magical painting with the world. It's the last step in the music-making process where a skilled engineer polishes the sound of a song to make it shine brightly. Just as an artist adds finishing touches to their masterpiece, mastering improves the sound of the music. It's like giving the music a magical makeover, making sure every note sounds its best and that it's ready to enchant listeners everywhere. So, mastering is like the final touch that brings out the full beauty and brilliance of a song.

64 - MASTER RIGHTS

Master rights are like owning the first copy ever of a magical book. They give the musician or record company special control over the very first recording of a song. It's like having the key to a safe that holds the purest form of the music. With master rights, you can decide how the recording is used, like selling it, licensing it or whether you want it to be played on the radio or in movies. Just like how the author of a book decides who gets to publish it, owning master rights means having the power to share the music with the world the way you want to. Master rights are like the ownership of the heart and soul of a song which is the recording of the music.

65 - MECHANICAL ROYALTIES

Imagine you're a builder in a magical kingdom, and every time someone uses one of your blueprints to build something, you get a little bit of treasure. Well, mechanical royalties are like that treasure, but for musicians!

In the music world, when someone makes a copy of a song, like putting it on a CD or even streaming it online, the musician who wrote that song gets a little bit of money. It's like getting a tiny bit of treasure in your piggy bank every time someone listens to your music.

These royalties are called "mechanical" because they come from when a copy is made of the music for someone to listen to. It's a bit like a magical machine that churns out copies of your favorite songs. So, whether you're listening to music you got at the record store, streaming it on your favorite app, or even singing it at a karaoke party, you're helping to fill the musician's treasure chest with little pieces of mechanical royalties. Like when you save your pennies, Mechanical Royalties can add up nicely.

66 - MEET & GREET

A meet & greet is like a special gathering where fans have the chance to meet their favorite musicians in person, like meeting legendary heroes from a magical tale. It's a chance for fans to connect with the artists they admire, sharing stories, hugs, and even taking photos together. Meet & greets often take place before or after concerts. Just as knights gather to celebrate their victories with their loyal subjects, musicians gather with their fans to express gratitude and share moments of joy. So, a meet & greet is like a little party where fans and musicians get together, creating unforgettable memories for everyone.

67 - MERCH

Merch, short for merchandise, is like a treasure chest of souvenirs and keepsakes that fans can collect to remember their musical adventures forever. It's like stepping into a mystical market filled with trinkets and treasures adorned with the symbols and logos of their favorite bands and artists. Merch can be many things like T-shirts, hats, posters, and even magical charms, each carrying a piece of the musical journey they represent. Some Merch might be special where you can only get it if you go to a concert. Some merch might even be only for their special fanclub to buy. Just as adventurers collect mementos from their travels, fans collect merch to celebrate their love for music and create memories of concerts and experiences. You can even get merchandise for avatars in games. Merch is like the enchanted loot that fans gather to carry the magic of music with them wherever they go.

68 - METADATA

Metadata is like a log book kept by discovery sailors, with the details of each musical voyage
that helps them on their next adventure. In music every song has metadata.

 Metadata is the very important information like the song's title, artist's name, album title, release
date, and genre, serving as a compass to navigate the vast sea of musical offerings. Just as
sailors record their journeys in logbooks, metadata catalogs the details of each musical piece in
digital libraries and 'databases'. Each song everywhere has its own metadata which helps
people all around the world find that one song. Metadata can help find other songs you might
like too that share the same genre like Pop or even similar lyrics. Did you know every song has
a special code called an ISRC. That is an International Standard Recording Code which is in the
metadata. There are so many songs in the world, the ISRC can help people find it on computers
quickly. So, metadata acts as the navigational chart for discovery sailors, guiding them through
the vast expanse of musical oceans and helping them uncover new treasures with greater ease.

69 - METAVERSE

The metaverse is like a magical place where the digital and real
worlds come together, much like a secret garden where
imagination blooms and real life mixes with make believe. It's a
digital universe where anybody can meet, play together, create,
and explore in ways that were once only possible in dreams. The
Metaverse gets better and better every day and even adults learn
something new about it all the time. It is a place we can all learn
together and you might already know lots about it.

In the metaverse, you can visit virtual worlds, play games, attend
concerts, and even build your own virtual home, much like
exploring alien planets or sailing the seas with squids. It's like
stepping into a portal to endless possibilities, where you can be
anyone and do anything your heart desires. Online worlds and
games like fortnite, Roblox and Horizon Worlds are all part of the
metaverse. The metaverse is like a magical playground where
imagination knows no bounds, inviting you to unleash your creativity and explore new horizons,
whether your avatar is battling aliens, befriending bears, or flying starships through the cosmos.
Oh yeah, the metaverse is also a great place to discover new music. People are watching virtual
concerts, buying virtual merchandise and listening to their favorite music in the metaverse every
day. It is a great place for new fans to find your music.

70 . MICRO-SYNC ROYALTIES

Micro-sync royalties are like tiny rewards that musicians receive when their music is used in short video snippets, like a few seconds of a song in a commercial or a quick clip in a TV show, much like finding little surprises hidden in unexpected places. It's like receiving a small token of appreciation for the contribution of your music to brighten up a moment or scene.

In the world of music licensing, micro-sync royalties are payments made to artists when their music is 'licensed' for short uses in different types of media, like background music in online videos or a little soundtrack for mobile games. Micro sync royalties can come from when music is mixed with video or images in online platforms like Instagram, Facebook, YouTube, or TikTok, which have 'user-generated' videos. Songs may only be used for a few seconds but the royalties can add up over time, like collecting coins dropped along a path.

Just as how every little bit counts when you're saving up for something special, micro-sync royalties provide a steady little stream of money for musicians. Micro-sync royalties are like the tiny treasures that add up to make a big difference in the lives of musicians, rewarding them for the magic they bring to countless moments in our daily lives.

71 - MIDDLE 8

The middle 8 is like the surprise in a story or a puzzle piece that makes the music extra exciting. It's a special part of a song where the song seems to change up a bit, like a twist in a fairy tale. Just when you think you know what's coming next, the middle 8 adds a fun surprise that makes the song even more interesting. It usually comes around the middle of the song to help mix it up a little. It's called the middle 8 because the change in music usually happens for 8 'bars'. A bar is just a measure of how many beats which you learn all about if you take music lessons. So, a Middle 8 is like a magical detour in the music that keeps you dancing and guessing or on the edge of your seat. Oh yeah, the Middle 8 might be the 'hook' of the song too.

72 - MIXING DESK

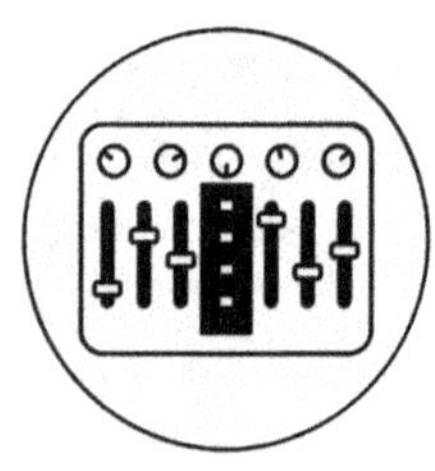

A mixing desk is like the control center where sound engineers weave their musical magic. It's a big board covered in knobs, sliders, and buttons that lets them mix together all the different sounds of a song. Imagine it's like the cockpit of a spaceship, with the engineer as the captain, navigating through the layers of music to create the perfect sonic journey. Remember the Input List from earlier?. Using the mixing desk, sound engineers can adjust the volume, balance, and effects of each instrument and voice, blending them together into a cool mix of sound. The mixing desk is like the tool that transforms individual musical channels into a magical musical masterpiece.

73 - MONITORS

Monitors are speakers positioned on stage, projecting sound back to the musicians. They make sure musicians can hear themselves and each other clearly during a loud performance. They're like amplifiers that send back the music being played just like In-Ear Monitors from before. Musicians rely on monitors to hear their vocals, instruments, and the mixture of the whole band, just like how you might use speakers to listen to your favorite songs in your room. Monitors help the musicians play the music just right, allowing performers to stay in sync and deliver an enchanting performance. Monitors are speakers that help guide musicians on their musical journey, ensuring they stay on track and create magical moments on stage.

74 - MUSIC BLOGGER

A music blogger is like a friendly storyteller, sharing exciting tales and discoveries about music, much like a cheerful explorer uncovering hidden gems in the jungle. They're like a good friend who guides you through the world of music, like a helpful compass pointing the way on a grand adventure.

A music blogger writes articles, reviews, and posts about music, sharing their passion and knowledge with others, much like a colorful guidebook that leads travelers to exciting destinations. Just as a storyteller captivates listeners with their tales, a music blogger captivates readers with news, recommendations, and glimpses into music and bands. Sometimes a Music Blogger might also be called a Music Journalist. Sometimes you might not like some of the music that a music blogger said was really good, everyone has their own different tastes and opinions. You can always choose whether you agree with a music blogger or not and follow them if you like them.

Whether introducing new artists or sharing concert experiences, music bloggers serve as a bridge between artists and fans, connecting people through their shared love of music.

75 - MUSIC CHARTS

Music charts are like maps that show which songs are the most popular. They are lists compiled by organizations that add up things like sales, streams, and radio airplay, like a leaderboard in a game where the best players rise to the top.

In the world of music, music charts are like snapshots of what people like right this minute much like a snapshot captures a moment in time. These are called 'trends', they're a reflection of what people are listening to and enjoying. News about the Music Charts might come out every week, every month or even every year like 'the most popular songs of the whole year'

Music lovers can use charts to discover new songs and artists, staying up-to-date with the latest hits. Music charts can be a tool for artists and listeners but don´t worry if your music is not in the Music Charts. There are far too many songs out there for all of them to be in music charts and there are plenty of people who will like your music even if it's not in the charts..

76 - MUSIC CRITIC

A music critic is like a wise owl who listens carefully to songs and then shares their thoughts about them with others, much like a storyteller who tells tales about adventures in far-off lands. They're a bit like a detective who explores every note and melody, searching for the secrets hidden within the music.

A music critic writes reviews and articles about songs and albums, sharing their opinions with readers, much like a guide who points out interesting things along a journey. Music Critics are much like Music Bloggers, but they usually write more about songs and albums, telling what they really think about it. They help people discover new music and understand what makes it special, like a treasure map that leads to musical gems. A music critic might have lots of people that look up to them and really like their opinion.
Just like Music Bloggers though, they can´t like every bit of music that people send to them. It is nice when a Music Critic likes your songs but that is their own opinion. Musicians don't make music just to keep music critics happy.

Just as a storyteller captivates listeners with their tales, a music critic captivates readers with their reviews in magazines, blogs and on websites.

77 - MUSIC EXPORT OFFICE

A Music Export Office is like a gateway that helps musicians share their music with audiences around the world. A Music Export Office provides help and guidance to musicians wanting to bring their music to other countries. Like loading up a ship with food and water before a long voyage, an export office can help with getting your music listened to in other countries, touring questions, and meeting people from the other countries before you set sail. A Music Export Office guides musicians on their global quests, helping them navigate the seas of international music business and share their enchanting melodies with listeners far and wide.

78 - MUSIC GENRE

Think of music genres like different kinds of sweets in a candy store! Just like how you have different flavors of sweets, there are different types of music that people love. You might have a favorite pop star whose songs you love to sing and dance to? Well, that's one type of music called "pop." It's super catchy and fun to listen to.

Now, imagine there are other types of music, like country music, which might tell stories about cowboys and horses, and hip-hop, which has cool beats and rhymes that make you want to move your feet. Each type of music has its own special sound and style, kind of like how each candy in the store has its own taste and color. There are other genres like Rock, Reggae, Disco, Jazz, Funk, Grime, Punk, Classical, Electronic and many more.

So, just like how you pick your favorite candy at the store, people pick their favorite types of music to listen to. Sometimes you can hear songs with a mixture of genres like a mixture of flavors. Just like how you enjoy trying different candies to see which one you like best, you can explore different types of music to find the ones that make you happiest. It's like going on a magical adventure through the world of music, where there's always something new and exciting to discover.

79 - MUSICIAN

A musician is someone who plays music. It could be someone who sings songs, plays an instrument like a saxophone, guitar or drums, or even someone who makes music on a computer. They're like the wizards of sound, using their instruments to create melodies and rhythms that make us want to dance or sing along, just like when you play pretend and make up your own songs with your friends. Just because you picked up a guitar one time in a music store does not make you a musician though. To be a musician, you probably love music to start. You also need to be ready to practice your instrument or singing for hours and hours.

80 - MUSIC LAWYER

A music lawyer, or music solicitor helps musicians understand all the rules everyone has to follow to make sure things are fair and safe. They are much like a skilled wizard wielding a powerful wand to ward off dark forces. Music Lawyers help you make sure you don´t break any rules or get in trouble and they can help you read agreements too.

In the world of music, music lawyers are like knights in shining armor, much like valiant heroes defending their kingdom from injustice. They work with agreements, contracts, copyrights, and many other legal things. Similar to how a beacon guides ships safely to harbor, music lawyers navigate the treacherous waters of the music business, guiding musicians through legal challenges and ensuring their rights are upheld. Thus, a music lawyer is more than just a legal advisor, they're a trusted protector, fighting tirelessly to uphold justice and fairness in the music business world.

81 - MUSIC STORE

A music store is like a castle filled with musical wonders, where you can find all sorts of instruments and more, like a toy store but for music. It's a place where you can discover guitars, drums, pianos, and all kinds of other instruments that make beautiful sounds.

In a music store, you can also find things like sheet music, which is like a map that shows you how to play your favorite songs on an instrument. You can also find things like guitar picks, guitar strings, violin strings, drumsticks, horns, books about music and music stands; all to help you make the most of your musical adventures.

Just like how a toy store is full of toys waiting to be played with, a music store is full of instruments waiting to make music. The people who work in music stores are sometimes happy to help you with any questions you have too. Visiting a music store is like going on a journey through the world of music.

82 - MUSIC SUPERVISOR

Imagine you're the director of a new movie, and you need the right soundtrack of songs to bring your story to life. Well, a music supervisor is like your advisor, helping you choose the perfect songs and music to set the mood and bring out the magic of your film.

In the world of movies, Games and TV shows, a music supervisor is a creative person who is responsible for selecting and licensing the music to be used. They work with directors, producers, and composers to find the perfect music for each scene and they get permission to use the music they pick as well.

From epic soundtracks to catchy tunes, music supervisors have a good ear for finding the right music to match the emotion, energy, and atmosphere of a scene in a film or on TV. They're like the conductors of an orchestra, ensuring that every note and melody enhances the story and captivates the audience.

So, whether you're watching a fast action movie or a sad moment between characters, you can thank the music supervisor for weaving their magic and making the music soundtrack an unforgettable part of the experience.

83 - MUSIC VIDEO DIRECTOR

A music video director is like a super cool creator who makes awesome videos with music and cool short clips you can watch called 'Visuals'. Just like the people who make those fun videos and games you love to watch and play online, a music video director mixes music with videos to make something really exciting and fun.

A music video director takes a song you like and turns it into a video story that you can watch, full of cool scenes and effects that match the music, kind of like watching your favorite cartoons or playing a cool video game. They use cameras and special tricks to make the music come alive on the screen, just like the cool effects you see in your favorite online videos and games.

So, a music video director is like the awesome creator who brings music to life with videos, making it even more fun for you to enjoy your favorite songs.

84 - NEIGHBORING RIGHTS

In the music world, neighboring rights are another special way to protect the people who made the song like the singers, musicians and songwriters. They're like a shield that helps them get paid when their music is played on the radio, in public places like restaurants or shops, or even in cinemas or on radio on the internet.

Imagine you have a magical umbrella that protects you when you're playing with your toys in your backyard. Well, neighboring rights are like that umbrella, but for musicians and their music.

Neighboring Rights make sure musicians get some credit and a little reward back. Like saying thank you for making awesome music and letting us hear it in a restaurant or at a store, even if you hear the song in a different country.

So, whether you're dancing to your favorite song in a club or hearing it play on the radio while you're driving, neighboring rights ensure that the performers and recording artists behind the music are recognized and rewarded for their magical talent.

85 - OVERDUB

An overdub is like adding layers of sounds onto a recording of music, like painting colorful strokes onto a canvas to create a masterpiece. It's a technique where new tracks are recorded over other tracks already recorded, like adding layers of frosting to a delicious cake.

In the world of audio production, overdubbing is like a sculptor shaping clay letting musicians experiment with different sounds and textures. Adding new sounds to your song or changing the sound of the guitar can be done by adding an overdub when recording. A singer doesn't have to sing at the same time a band is recording their music. They could do overdubs later to record vocal bits.

Similar to how a chef adds spices to enhance the flavor of a dish, overdubs enrich the sound of the music. Overdubbing is more than just a technical process, it's a creative tool that allows artists to express themselves fully and bring their musical visions to life even more.

86 - OVERHEADS

Overheads are the microphones that capture the entire sound of a drum kit from up above. That is why they are called overheads because they are usually over the drummer's head. They're placed high up and spread out over the drums, like birds soaring in the sky, capturing every detail of the music. In a recording studio or at concerts, overheads pick up the shimmering cymbals, the thunderous toms, and the crisp snare drum, blending them all together into a symphony of sound. It's like having another pair of ears that can hear every whisper and roar of the drums, creating a rich sound.

87 - PERCUSSIONS

Percussion is like the heartbeat of a jungle, pulsing with energy and bringing the rhythm of the natural world to life with all it´s sounds.

In the world of music, percussion is all about making sounds with instruments that you hit, shake, or scrape. It's like being a musical scientist discovering new things to bang on like drums or shake like a tambourine.

From booming drums to shimmering cymbals, percussion instruments come in all shapes and sizes, each adding its own unique flavor to the music. It's like an orchestra of sounds, working together to create rhythms that make you want to dance. Some special drums and even bells come from cultures far away and have their own sound like nothing else you have heard before. There are even little shakers that look like eggs with pebbles, rice or beads inside that make a loud sound when you shake them, almost like a rattlesnake. Those ones are actually called egg shakers.

Whether you're tapping your feet to a funky beat or shaking a tambourine in a parade, percussion is your guide, leading you on a rhythmic journey through the wild world of music.

88 - PER DIEMS

Per diems are like special coins that musicians get when they're away from home for a concert or many concerts in a row, which is called a 'tour'. A band might have a tour of the United States, Canada or even all of Europe when they do many shows together and can be away from home for a long time. Per diems are money they use to buy food and other things they need while they're traveling. It's like getting a weekly allowance from your parents except the Tour Manager or Tour Accountant will usually give it to them. Imagine you're on a camping trip, and your parents give you coins to buy snacks at the store. Per diems work the same way but for grown-up musicians when they're on tour. So, it's like having a little stash of coins to buy snacks and souvenirs while exploring new places.

89 - PERFORMING RIGHTS

Performing rights are like another shield that protects songwriters, musicians and creators, making sure they receive fair credit and rewards whenever their music is played in public. It is like a big thumbs-up when their songs get played on the radio, at concerts or even in movies or TV Shows. It's like saying "Hey, your music is awesome so we´re going to play it for everyone to enjoy. Performance royalties are the little gift they get when their music is played. These are collected by performing rights organizations, serving as the guardians of creativity, safeguarding the livelihoods of musicians and creators by ensuring they get their due rewards for their magical melodies and enchanting performances.

90 - PERFORMING RIGHTS ORGANISATION (PRO)

A Performing Rights Organisation (PRO) is another guardian of music, ensuring that songwriters and composers are fairly paid for their creations. They hold a magical shield that protects the rights of musicians, allowing them to earn royalties whenever their music is performed in front of people. PROs collect fees from concert venues, Radio Stations, and online platforms that use music, then share those royalties to the artists. Kind of like collecting club fees to be able to play music. Imagine them as the defenders of creativity, standing up for musicians and ensuring they receive fair rewards for their work. Just as knights protect their kingdom, PROs safeguard the livelihoods of musicians, allowing them to continue sharing their magic with the world. A Performing Rights Organisation is like a noble guardian, upholding the rights and dignity of music creators everywhere.

91 - PERFORMANCE ROYALTIES

Performance royalties are the magical rewards that musicians receive when their music is played or performed in public where there are people, much like receiving a gift for sharing something special with others. Royalties are the treasure thrown into the treasure chest every time your music is heard on the radio, in a concert, or even in a restaurant. They might be a small number of coins but the Performance Rights Organization will help collect them from everywhere, all over the world. Just like how even pennies can fill up a piggy bank, performance royalties can grow.

It's like getting a little prize each time your music brings joy to someone's ears. Performance royalties are like the magical tokens of appreciation that remind musicians of the power of their music to touch hearts and inspire minds, making every performance a truly enchanting experience.

92 - PHYSICAL DISTRIBUTION

Physical distribution started in the days of old and is still with us today. Just like brave knights would protect pilgrims traveling to other lands, music would get from the recording studio safely into the eager hands of listeners. 'Physical' is a word that helps describe something you can hold in your hands or touch, not just stream on your computer or phone.

Music can be made and delivered to you in many ways or 'formats' like CD´s, vinyl records, or things like cassettes, which your grandparents might remember. Record Labels would distribute them in big trucks or vans to record stores where fans would go, excited for the moment they could hold them in their hands like prized possessions. Physical distribution is like the noble quest undertaken by valiant knights, ensuring that the treasure of these musical products reaches its destination safely, to be enjoyed and cherished by all who seek its enchanting melodies.

93 - PHYSICAL PRODUCT

A physical product is the treasure that you can hold in your hands, much like a shiny gemstone that sparkles in the sunlight. It is something that you can see, touch, and feel.

In the world of music a physical product can mean a lot of things these days. Physical products can be things like CD´s, Cassettes, Vinyl Albums, and can even come with other merchandise like Music Books, T-Shirts, Hats & much more.

A playlist is like a special mix of your favorite songs, carefully chosen and put together to create the perfect 'soundtrack', much like picking out your favorite ingredients to make a delicious meal. It is your personal collection of songs that you can change to fit your mood, whether you're feeling happy, sad, or ready to dance. Your parents might remember calling them a 'Mixtape', when they would share songs on a cassette with friends and family.

In a playlist, you can gather all sorts of songs that you love, arranging them in a way that flows smoothly from one song to the next, like putting together pieces of a puzzle to create a beautiful picture. Whether you're looking for songs to relax with, songs to run to, or songs to sing along with, a playlist has something for every moment and mood.

Just like how you feel excited and energized when you have all your favorite toys or games ready to play, listening to a playlist can bring that same feeling of joy as you dive into the music you love.

95 - PRODUCER

A music producer is like the director of a movie, guiding the creation of new music from start to finish. They work very closely with the band or artist, helping them shape their songs, choose the right instruments and sounds, and bring their musical vision to life. It's like having a wise wizard by your side, using their skill to make the music sound its best. Just as a director oversees a film's production, a music producer oversees every detail of a song's creation. So, a producer is like the mastermind behind the scenes, weaving together all the elements to create musical magic.

96 - PRODUCTION MANAGER

A production manager is like a captain of a ship, steering the crew through the turbulent seas of a live concert to bring forth amazing shows, like a skilled navigator guiding a ship through stormy waters. They're like the leader of a symphony, orchestrating the group of artists and technicians to create mesmerizing performances. A production manager oversees everything in a concert production, making sure that the show sails smoothly from start to finish, much like a captain ensures the safe passage of their vessel to its destination. Artists and technicians rely on the production manager to guide them through the challenges of bringing their visions to life. When you see things at concerts like parts of a stage moving or someone flying through the air, it is the production manager who makes sure it can be done. From building the stage to making sure all the lights are working and all the equipment arrived safely, the Production Manager has a very busy job to do.

97 - PRODUCTION MUSIC WRITER

A production music writer is like a musical architect, building adventures with sound and melodies for all kinds of stories, and scenes, much like a master builder creating giant castles and towering cities. They are creative wizards who weave melodies and rhythms into enchanting spells that set the mood and bring scenes to life.

A production music writer creates special music for things like movies, TV shows, and commercials, crafting melodies and arrangements that fit perfectly with the action and emotions on screen, much like a tailor sewing costumes to fit the characters in a play. They help create the atmosphere and mood of a scene, like a painter adding colors to a canvas to evoke feelings and emotions. Just as a master builder constructs buildings from bricks and mortar, a production music writer constructs musical landscapes from notes and rhythms. Some musicians just make production music and don´t play live concerts.

98 - PROMOTER

A promoter spreads the excitement and energy of a concert or event. They're the ones who make sure people know about the show and come to experience the magic of live music. Imagine them as the ringmaster of a circus, inviting everyone to the spectacle under the big top. Promoters work very hard to advertise the event, sell tickets, and create an exciting buzz around the performers. It is the promoters job to make sure people hear about a show or concert before it happens. Just as a conductor guides the musicians through a symphony, a promoter guides the audience through a night of musical enchantment, creating unforgettable experiences for everyone.

99 - PROMOTER REP

A promoter rep is like a friendly helper who works behind the scenes to make sure everyone knows about exciting events and shows, kind of like the people who help spread the word about cool new games or toys you might want to play with. They are the cheerful messenger who helps share news about fun things happening in your neighborhood.

A promoter rep's job is to talk to people and let them know about upcoming concerts, shows, and events, just like how your friend might tell you about a cool party happening soon. They use social media, emails, and other ways to spread the word and get people excited, much like how you share fun stuff with your friends online. When the day of the concert arrives, sometimes promoters will have more than one show or concert on the same day. Just like a trusty friend, they might send someone to take their place and represent them. The Promoter Rep will help the tour manager, production manager and band put on a great show. That is where the name promoter rep comes from, Promoter Representative.

So, a promoter rep is like the friendly helper who brings people together to enjoy awesome music and makes sure the whole concert runs smoothly.

100 - PR PERSON

A PR person is short for Public Relations person. They are like storytellers who weave enchanting tales about musicians and their music. They are skilled artisans crafting masterpieces of stories, using words and images to paint pictures of artists and their musical journey. A PR person shouts out about musicians and their work to the world, sharing their stories, music, and projects through newspapers, magazines, radio, TV interviews, and social media, much like a herald announcing the arrival of a noble knight to the kingdom. PR people share stories that excite fans and spark their interest in the magic of music. A PR person is the messenger who spreads the word about musicians far and wide, connecting them with fans and followers who eagerly await their next musical adventure.

101 - PUBLISHING RIGHTS

Publishing rights are like having a special treasure map that shows who owns the words and melodies of a song, how the music flows. It's like being the guardian of the storybook of music, deciding who gets to share its tales with the world. When someone owns publishing rights, they have the power to decide how the song is used, like if it's played on the radio, used in movies, or printed in sheet music so other people can learn how to play the songs. Just like how an author decides who can print and sell their book, owning publishing rights means having control over how the song's story is told and shared. Publishing rights are like the guardianship of a song's words and creative journey.

102 - P WITH A CIRCLE AROUND IT (℗)

The "P with a circle around it" is like a secret badge that shows who owns the recording of a song. It's like putting a special mark on your favorite toy to show that it's yours. When you see the "P with a circle around it," it means that someone owns the recording of the music, like the band or their record company. The recording of the song can be made in a recording studio or even at home in your bedroom on a computer. They have special rights to decide how the recording is used and who can use it. So, it's like a magical stamp that helps keep track of who owns the music recording, just like marking your territory on a special map.

103 - RECORDING STUDIO

A recording studio is like a bustling workshop where musicians craft their music, like a busy kitchen where chefs create tasty dishes. It's a special space where musical ideas grow and take flight, much like an artist's studio where vibrant paintings come to life. In a recording studio, musicians use special equipment and technology to capture their music talents, layering sounds and melodies to weave song compositions, much like skilled ceramic makers sculpting fine pottery. Just as artisans rely on their tools to shape clay into works of art, musicians rely on recording studios to transform their musical ideas into reality. Many times a band will record their music in a studio with a Producer who uses the equipment to help them shape the music.

104 - RECORD LABEL

Imagine you're the captain of a starship in space, discovering new sounds and artists on every planet you visit along the way. Pretend it is your job to pick the best music you find and spread the joy to all the other planets, even if the music is something they have never heard of before. Well, a record label is like your trusty crew, guiding the ship and helping the musicians you pick up navigate the journey with you.

In the world of music, a record label is like a company that works with musicians to produce, promote, and distribute their music by spreading it all around. It's like having a whole team behind the scenes, using their skills to bring your musical dreams to life.

Record labels can help musicians record their songs in studios, make eye-catching artwork and album covers, and get their music out into the world through stores, streaming platforms, radio stations & more. They're like the guardians of your musical journey, helping you navigate the highs and lows of the music business. Whether you are on your own as a solo artist or a band with dreams of making it big, a record label can be like your musical home, a place where you can work with the people there who believe in you and like your music. Not every musician has a record label to work with and some choose to do everything on their own with some help from other companies called 'label services'. Record labels can be a great home for your music and help you the best when you really like the people that work there. Remember, it is your music if you made it so you can choose whether or not a record label is the best thing for you.

105 - REHEARSALS

Rehearsals are like practice sessions for a concert performance or a tour you might be doing soon. It's good to have rehearsals before going to the recording studio to record songs as well. Rehearsals are where the band gets together to make sure everything sounds perfect. It's like when you and your friends practice riding your bikes together or have football practice or dance rehearsals. During rehearsals, musicians fine-tune their songs, work on their moves, and make sure they're all in sync, just like the dancers practicing their steps before a recital. Small bands, solo artists and big bands should all have rehearsals to be the best they can be. You can rehearse in a rehearsal studio or even at home if the neighbors don´t mind the noise. Rehearsals are like the secret behind-the-scenes practice that makes the magic happen on stage and in the studio.

106 - REHEARSAL STUDIO

A rehearsal studio can feel like a secret club or hideout where musicians gather to fine-tune their craft, much like a cozy den where friends come together to play and explore without lots of other people around watching them. It's a space that has instruments, amplifiers, and isn't too noisy for the neighbors. Usually rehearsal studios have special material on the walls to keep the loud noise inside when the doors are shut. That material is called soundproofing.

In the world of music, a rehearsal studio is where bands and artists practice their skills and prepare for performances. It's a place where melodies are born, harmonies are perfected, and musical ideas come to life, resembling a workshop where dreams take shape.

Similar to how athletes train in a gym to improve their skills, musicians gather in rehearsal studios to practice their instruments, and play together with fellow bandmates. A rehearsal studio serves as an important hub for musicians, offering a space where they can unleash their creativity, perfect their performances, and embark on musical journeys together.

107 - RHYTHM SECTION

The rhythm section is like the sturdy foundation of a castle, providing the solid ground upon which the musical kingdom is built. It is where the bass and drums mix like roots and branches, creating a balance of power and grace. The rhythm section starts with both the drummer and the bass player setting the heartbeat of the music, driving the groove and laying the groundwork for melodies to soar with it´s rhythmic flow. Just as the earth's core provides stability to the planet, the rhythm section grounds the music in rhythm and harmony, so that the melodies dance joyfully above. When the bass player and the drummer listen to each other closely, the other musicians can have an easier time following the beat. The bass player and drummer work closely together to keep the beat in time creating a great rhythm section.

108 - RIDER

A rider is like a wish list for the band. It's a list of special things they would like backstage before a concert, like their favorite snacks, drinks, or even decorations for their dressing room. The promoter is sent the rider weeks before the show to give them enough time to prepare. It can be hard being away from home or having to wait for hours to play so the rider has some things they like to make them happy. It's like writing a letter to Santa Claus, but instead of asking for toys, they're asking for things to make them feel comfortable and happy before they go on stage. A Rider doesn't have to be full of silly expensive things, some bands ask for things like water, juice, fruit and even coloring books with crayons or local postcards that they can send home to family.

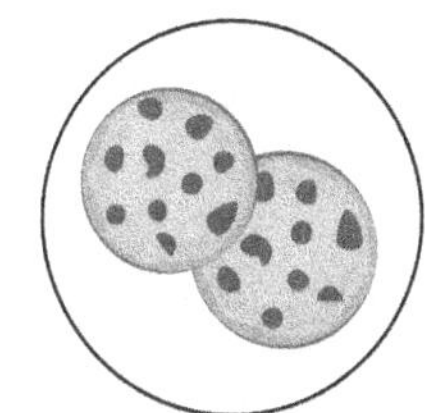

109 - RIGHTS HOLDER

A rights holder is like the guardian of a treasure chest, protecting the valuable rights to music, movies, or other creative works. It is another name for the keeper of the keys, responsible for overseeing how these treasures are shared and used. A rights holder owns the copyrights or license to a piece of 'creative content', granting them the power to control how it is spread. It's like being the guardian of a precious artifact, ensuring that it's treated with care and respect. Just as guardians safeguard their treasures from harm, rights holders protect the creative works they are responsible for.

110 - ROADIE

A roadie is like a super helper for the band. They're the ones who make sure everything is set up perfectly for a concert, like setting up instruments, lights, and sound equipment. They're like invisible backstage wizards who make sure the stage is ready for the band to perform their magic. Imagine they're like the crew in a Navy ship, working together to prepare for an epic adventure. In fact, another name for roadies sometimes is 'crew' and the production manager and tour manager work together to find the best crew they can. So, roadies are like the unsung heroes behind the scenes, making sure everything runs smoothly so the band can rock.

111 - ROOMLIST

In the music business, a roomlist is like a secret list that tells everyone in the band which rooms they'll stay in when they're traveling for concerts, just like when you go on a big adventure and everyone gets their own special room in a hotel. It helps everyone know where they'll sleep and where to find each other, kind of like having a secret code to unlock the mystery of where everyone is staying. A Roomlist is also a great tool for the Tour Manager to find you if you accidentally sleep in too late.

112 - ROYALTIES

Royalties are like special treats that musicians get when their music is played or used, it is a way they make some money. It's like getting a small prize every time someone listens to your favorite song on the radio or watches a movie where your music is featured. Remember we already learned about mechanical royalties, performance royalties, micro-sync royalties and more?. Imagine it's like receiving a little gift in the mail every time your artwork is displayed in a museum. Royalties are like a thank-you from the people who use your music, giving you a little something in return for sharing your talent with the world. Royalties can be very small but they can fill your piggy bank up quickly sometimes. It's like getting a reward for bringing joy to people's ears with your music.

113 - SAMPLES

Samples are like ingredients borrowed from your favorite dishes to create new culinary delights. They're like collecting colorful beads from different jars to craft a unique necklace. In music, samples are snippets of sound taken from songs or recordings you know already. The samples are then used by musicians to add texture, flavor, and depth to their own songs. Just as chefs blend various ingredients to create a masterpiece, musicians can blend samples with their own songs to produce captivating melodies and rhythms. Sometimes artists use sounds from other musicians' songs because they really like it. Maybe they will use a little bit of the guitar riff for instance. Remember though, even your parents need to ask for permission when they use samples of other people's songs. Sometimes you aren't allowed to use sampled pieces of music from other people's songs. The artist you borrow a sample of music from needs to receive some royalties too since they wrote that bit of music. Like borrowing a toy, you must ask the person who owns the toy.

114 - SCORE

A score is like a map that guides musicians through a musical journey, showing them the notes and rhythms they need to play to create beautiful melodies and harmonies. It's like a blueprint filled with musical symbols and markings, showing them what to play. A score gives instructions for each instrument so they can play together. Just as explorers rely on maps, musicians rely on scores to navigate through a piece of music. You might hear somebody say that they did 'the score' for a film.

115 - SESSION MUSICIAN

A session musician is like a scientist who is really good at using their skills and knowledge. They are some of the best musicians in the land that other bands can pay to come and play with them. They're like mystical travelers who journey through different realms of music, lending their skills to different musical projects. Session musicians are paid money to perform on recordings or live performances by other artists, adding their own unique touch to the music. Session musicians use their expertise to lift the songs they play on, whether it's adding a beautiful guitar riff or a amazing drum beat. A session musician brings their magical talents to every musical adventure they embark on.

116 - SHOWCASE

A showcase is like a special concert where musicians sometimes perform their music in front of music industry professionals, like talent scouts, record label people, and managers. During a showcase, artists have the opportunity to shine and impress these industry people, who can help with their careers and open doors to new exciting opportunities. Sometimes bands will play at showcase conferences in other countries so they can play in front of important music industry people in that country. Maybe a Music Export office in your own country can help you get invited to a showcase festival in another country. It's like taking a giant leap forward on the path to musical success, with every note played and every song sung helping the artist's journey. So, a showcase is like a golden opportunity for musicians to show their skills and take their careers to new heights.

117 - SOUNDCHECK

Before a concert, the band makes sure all the instruments and microphones sound perfect by playing some songs together. It's like when you check if your toys are all set up before you start playing with them. Soundchecks happen before the public comes in and the concert starts. Sometimes bands invite special fans to come and watch the soundcheck as a treat or a thank you for being a superfan. It's 'all hands on deck' for the soundcheck. Both the crew and band make sure everything is ready for the show later.

118 - SOUND ENGINEER

A sound engineer is like a wise owl who controls the magic of sound during a concert. They're the ones who make sure the music sounds just right, setting the volume, balance, and special effects. It's like they have a magical wand that can make the music louder or softer, clearer or with more effects, depending on what's needed. Imagine they're like the conductor of an orchestra, guiding each instrument to create a beautiful melody. So, sound engineers are like the magicians who bring the music to life with their technical expertise and skill.

119 - SPLIT SHEET

A split sheet is like when friends put a puzzle together. Some friends might find more pieces than other friends. Just like the Pirate code divides up the booty from a great adventure at sea, a Split Sheet is a list that helps musicians and songwriters share the treasure of a song fairly. It is an agreement that makes sure everyone who helped put the song together gets their fair share of recognition and rewards.

In a split sheet, all the makers of a song, like the lyricists, composers, and performers, are listed along with their share of the ownership, much like marking each adventurer's share of the treasure. It helps make sure that everyone involved in creating the magic of a song receives their rightful split of royalties and credits. One member of a band might receive a bigger amount, or percentage, because they wrote more of the song than another member did.

Like Pirates are told how much of the booty they will get before setting sail, it is best for all your band mates to agree how much share each person gets before the song is released to the world.

120 - STAGE DESIGNER

Have you ever gone to a big concert or a grand show where the whole stage looked like it was from a movie?. A stage designer might have had something to do with it. They are like architects of dreams, crafting fantastical worlds where performers come alive and stories unfold, much like a master storyteller creating magical kingdoms with words and imagination. They're creative professionals who design how the stage looks, like an artist painting vibrant scenes on a canvas of performance.

In the world of entertainment, a stage designer is like a magician performing illusions and enchantments. Like TV shows where they fix up people's homes, Stage Designers can take an ordinary stage and turn it into an extraordinary setting that captivates audiences' hearts and minds. They imagine and create stage layouts, lighting designs, and set pieces, resembling craftsmen sculpting the backdrop for a grand theatrical spectacle.

A stage designer guides the audience's gaze and emotions through the setting of a performance, creating moments of excitement that lasts long after the show finishes. A stage designer is more than just a creator of scenery, they help shape the magic of live entertainment for all to behold.

121 - STAGE MANAGER

A stage manager is like the conductor of an orchestra, knowing every detail behind the scenes to ensure that the show runs smoothly, much like a puppeteer guiding the strings of marionettes in a big theater. Stage Managers are in charge of everything unfolding on stage, coordinating the efforts of artists, technicians, and crew members with precision and grace. A stage manager is responsible for everything from setting up the stage to even telling performers when they need to start sometimes. They are like the right hand person of a Production Manager sometimes. Stage Managers are the keepers of time on stage. It is always best to do what they tell you to help them make the concert run smoothly.

122 - STAGE PLOT

If you were about to build a big house you would draw it on paper first like an architect does. A stage plot is like the plan or map that guides the crew when they set up the stage for a performance. It's a detailed blueprint that shows where each instrument, microphone, and piece of equipment should be placed. A stage plot helps make sure that everything is in its right place, allowing the performers to move smoothly during the show. Just as adventurers rely on maps to navigate through unknown lands, the crew relies on the stage plot to help set up the stage.

123 - STEMS

Stems are like the roots of plants that branch out from a song each carrying a unique part of the song's DNA, much like the branches of a tree spreading into the sky. Stems are single pieces of a song recording, like the vocals, drums, or guitars, mixed together, like flowers arranged in a colorful display.

In the world of audio production, stems are like building blocks that allow engineers to sculpt the sound to perfection, much like architects designing a majestic castle from stone and mortar. They're essential tools for remixing, editing, and building music, resembling a box of Lego bricks waiting to be assembled into a magnificent structure. An engineer or producer can take a whole song and just put the bass guitar together with the piano and nothing else. That would be called a 'stem'. Just like taking 2 slices away from a pizza.

Audio engineers use stems to control the balance and dynamics of a mix, weaving together different elements to create a blend of sound. The 'dynamics' are things like how loud or how quiet the music is. Sometimes you might hear a little bit of a song you know in a movie or on a commercial. It might just be the guitar, piano and drums you can hear without the singer but you recognize it. That would be a stem that the engineer or producer made from the recording. It can make you think of that song even if not all the instruments are there. Stems are the building blocks.

124 - STREAMING ROYALTIES

Streaming royalties are like coins collected by musicians every time their music is streamed (played) on streaming platforms (DSPs), much like that piggy bank that fills up with coins with each listen. They are payments made to artists and rights holders for the use of their music on platforms like Spotify, Apple Music, and YouTube. There are many other platforms like Spotify that your music can be streamed on all over the world and each one has special ways to help musicians get their music played more. There are streaming platforms like Deezer in France, Boomplay in Africa and as far as China and South Korea.

In the world of music, streaming royalties are like a reward that musicians get depending on the number of times their songs are streamed (listened to). They're an important way for some artists to make money, helping to support their careers and passion for making music.

Similar to how a river flows steadily, streaming royalties can provide a steady stream of money for musicians if people are listening. Bands sometimes still need to find ways to tell their fans that their music is on streaming platforms for them to listen to.

125 - SUBSCRIPTION SERVICES

Subscription services can be like having a music box that you can listen to any song you want to, any time you want to. Much like having a library card that lets you explore countless books but from the comfort of your home. Subscription Services can unlock doors to a world of movies, music, games, and more, all at your fingertips.

Subscription services allow you to pay a monthly amount of money to join the vast library of things to watch and listen to, like having a never-ending buffet of your favorite foods available whenever you want. People who pay the monthly subscription fee are called subscribers and get to uncover new experiences like songs they have never heard or films and games along the way. Subscription Services know when you have listened to your favorite song and will send the artist and rights holders some streaming royalties after you listened.

126 - SUPERFAN

A superfan is like a superhero friend who loves a band or musician more than anything else in the world. They know all the songs by heart, collect posters and merchandise, and go to every concert they can. It's like when you have a favorite toy or character that you love so much, you want everything else just like it. Superfans are like the biggest cheerleaders for the band, always supporting and cheering them on, like how your best friend supports you in everything you do. It is very important for a band or artist to pay good attention to their Superfans. Sometimes artists will let superfans come to their soundcheck or might even have a special secret video concert online for superfans only. Sometimes artists release a new song and only superfans who are in the fan club can hear the song first. They might even make T-Shirts that only fans in the fanclub can get. You can usually see if an artist or band has a special fanclub on their website.

127 - SUPPORT BAND

A support band are the talented performers who play before the main act at a concert, warming up the audience and getting everyone excited for the headline show. It is not any easy thing to do because the crowd is usually very excited to see their favorite artist play next. Support Bands are like a group of brave adventurers who join forces to conquer challenges together.

In the world of concerts, a support band is like a trusty sidekick who shares the stage with the headline band, adding their own flair and energy to the performance, much like a group of loyal bears standing by your side in times of need. They're the unsung heroes who entertain the crowd and set the mood for a night of musical enchantment. If you like the support band, they might even become one of your favorites too one day soon. Many support bands grow to be the main band on stage one day. It isn't an easy job getting more and more fans every day. Being a Support Band to a bigger artist gives you the chance to play in front of a bigger crowd of people and the chance of winning new fans. Just as how friends support each other through thick and thin, a support band lifts up the spirits of concert-goers and creates memories that last a lifetime.

128 - SYNC LICENSING

Sync licensing (or Licensing & Sync) is like giving permission for
your music to be used in movies, TV shows, commercials, or
video games. Sync (or Synch) is just a short word for
Synchronization'. That is when two or more things work together
at the same time like synchronized swimmers do in a swimming
pool. If two clocks or watches tell you different times, they are not
in sync. When a filmmaker or a game developer wants to use a
song in their project, they need to get a sync license from the
musician, rights holder or their representatives. It's like asking for
a special key to unlock the magic that the music will add to their
creation. When you watch a fast action superhero film, you might
hear fast music that makes you sit up in your seat. When you
watch a movie about someone that is going away for a long time
you might hear sad music. The music is in sync with what you are
watching and helps with the emotions or feeling of the scene. The
director, or someone called the Music Supervisor, looks for the
best music to use and will offer the artist and rightsholder some money to be able to use their
music. The Artist will sign a special agreement on paper which is called the license.

Sync Licensing is a great way for a musician, songwriters or bands to make extra money and
make new fans. Sometimes very big companies will pay lots of money to use a song that they
really like. Sometimes when people hear a song in a film, or in a game or in a TV advert, they
will search to see who the band is because they like the music. They might become new fans
and will even search for more of your music to listen to.

129 - TALENT SCOUT

A talent scout is like an expert explorer who travels far and wide in search of hidden talent,
much like a skilled detective who uncovers clues and solves mysteries. They're the sharp-eyed
observers who have a gift for discovering budding stars. Talent Scouts may work for record
labels (like A&R people), publishing companies or even TV Shows.

In the world of entertainment, a talent scout is like a mentor who guides artists on their path to
success, much like a trusted guide who leads travelers through new lands. When a good Talent
Scout finds you they will often help & give you advice and support along the way.

130 - TALKBACK

The word 'Talkback' sounds like when you don't agree with your parents and argue with them, but in music it is very different. Talkback is like a secret whisper device that connects musicians and sound engineers during a recording session so they can talk from different parts of the recording studio. It's a system that allows the recording engineer to speak to musicians in the studio through their headphones. Like being able to answer your front door and say "who is it? " through the intercom. In a live show at a concert, the sound engineer can use talkback to talk with the stage manager or crew behind the stage too.

131 - TEMPO

Tempo is like the heartbeat of music, setting the pace and rhythm for listeners to follow, much like the steady beat of a drum guiding dancers in a parade. It's the magical pulse that tells whether a song moves swiftly like a racehorse or slowly like a stroll in the park.

In music, tempo is the speed a piece of music is played or performed, like how fast or slow the hands of a clock move. It helps both the musicians and listeners feel the energy and flow of a song, whether it's upbeat and lively like a joyful dance or gentle like a lullaby.

The Tempo of a song can be measured just like a ruler can measure a line you draw. You measure the tempo of a song by how many beats there are every minute, like when you clap your hands to the beat of a song. The number of beats per minute (BPM) is the tempo of the song.

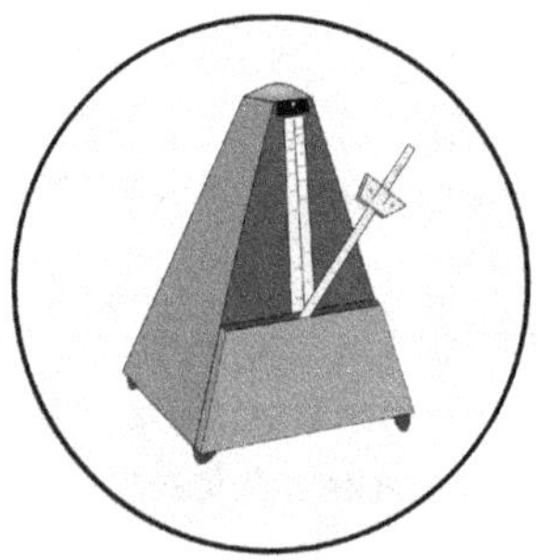

132 - TOUR ACCOUNTANT

A tour accountant is really good at numbers, making sure all the money for the music adventure is in order. Like a detective of money, they know how much is left in the pot when money has been spent .

They help with things like figuring out how much money is needed for the tour and keeping track of how much money there is, a bit like when we keep track of our toys or treats. They also make sure everyone knows where the money is going, so everyone can stay happy and focused on the hard work and fun of the tour. A tour accountant is super important for making sure everything goes smoothly.

133 - TOUR BUS DRIVER

A tour bus is like a giant magical house on wheels for the band when they're on tour. It's like a big moving castle where they sleep, eat, and hang out together while traveling from one city to the next one for concerts. Imagine it's like your own house on wheels, with bunk beds, a kitchen, and even a lounge area where everyone can relax and have fun. The Tour Bus Driver has the most important job ever; it is their job to get everyone to the next show safely. Tours may be for many days in a row with shows every night. The next city you need to go to might be very far away so in a tour bus you can sleep while you drive there. It's like having a home that travels with you, making every journey an adventure and it´s the bus driver that leads the way. Remember to say goodnight to your bus driver and it is always nice to ask them if they need something like water, they deserve some attention.

134 - TOUR MANAGER

Just as knights would lead their comrades into battle, tour managers lead their bandmates and crew through the ups and downs of touring, and playing concerts in different cities every day. Tour Managers are always ready to face any challenges that come their way, they are like the fearless leader who organizes every part of a band's journey on the road, ensuring smooth sailing from one concert venue to the next. A tour manager is responsible for many things like making sure there is enough time for everyone to do their work. They organize transportation like buses, cars and airplanes. Tour Managers also organize hotels, press, and budgets (money), and make sure that everything runs like clockwork. They're the ones who keep the tour on track, making sure the band is ready to rock the stage.

135 - TUBE AMP

A tube amp is a guitar amplifier, like a cauldron that brews the rich and warm tones that guitarists crave. It's like a secret recipe passed down from long ago which helps create a beautiful sound, making the guitar sound warm and fuzzy like a cozy blanket. A tube amp uses old vacuum tubes to amplify a signal from an electric guitar, which gives the sound a beautiful character. Just as baking cookies in the oven makes them smell and taste yummy, playing a guitar through a tube amp makes it sound awesome. Many guitar players love the sound that an old tube amplifier adds.

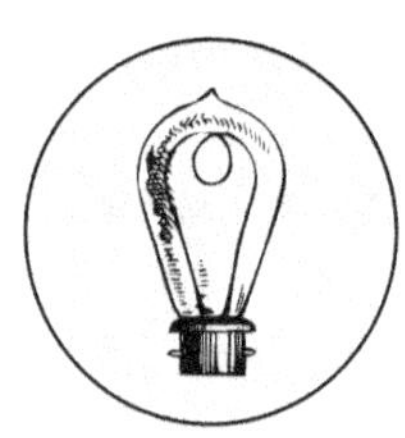

136 - TUNER

A tuner is like a compass for music, guiding you to the perfect pitch, much like a compass that helps you find your way through a forest. It's a special tool that helps musicians ensure their instruments are playing the right notes, whether they're tuning a guitar, piano, or even their voice.

In the world of music, a tuner listens to the sound of an instrument and shows if it's in tune or needs adjusting, like a friendly guide who points out the best path to take. On a guitar each string has its own musical note and a tuner will make sure it is the perfect note. It's like having a magical helper who whispers in your ear, ensuring every note you play is perfect.

Just as how sailors rely on the North Star to navigate the seas, musicians rely on tuners to steer their way through the melody, keeping them on course and in harmony with the music. So, a tuner is like a digital companion that helps you find your musical direction and keep you in tune.

137 - UNDERSCORE

An underscore is like a quiet friend in the background, adding to the fun without taking all the attention away, much like a shadow that follows you silently wherever you go. It's a bit of music that plays like a breeze of air adding excitement to something you are watching.

In the world of film and television, an underscore is like a hidden bit of music that weaves through the story, guiding your feelings, much like a skilled puppeteer moving marionettes behind the scenes. Composers craft clever underscores that keep you watching but they don´t take your attention away from the main action of a film. An underscore of music can be a very important part of storytelling in a film, like a silent guardian guiding the audience through the journey.

138 - USER GENERATED VIDEOS

User-generated videos are like movies created by people just like you at home or outside, capturing special moments. Even if it's a short video you make on your phone or when you share ideas with the world in a longer video, it is like crafting your own story or adventure to share with friends.

In the online world of computers, user-generated videos are videos made by people who are not professional filmmakers or directors. They can be about anything like funny clips, videos teaching people how to make something or anything you like to talk about. Platforms like Instagram, Facebook, YouTube, and TikTok are filled with these videos, which are fun to watch sometimes. On platforms like TikTok and Instagram you can add music to your user generated videos and people who watch it might like the music as well.

Just like how you might share drawings, stories, or games with your friends, creating and sharing user-generated videos is a way for people to connect, and share their stories with others. Making a funny short video and sharing it with one of your songs is a great way to get new fans of your music too.

139 - VIDEO GAME COMPOSER

A video game composer is someone who is really good at playing video games and making exciting music for the games they love to play, much like the talented storytellers who craft magical adventures for you to explore. They are musical architects who design the soundscape of a game, setting the mood and making it more fun to play.

A video game composer writes music that fits perfectly with the action of a game, just like a soundtrack that accompanies a thrilling movie. Whether it's epic battle themes, mysterious scary moments, or catchy tunes for happy moments, they use their creativity to bring the game world to life through music.

Just like how music adds excitement to your favorite movies or shows, the music created by a video game composer adds feelings to the games you play. A video game composer is like the maestro who orchestrates the soundtrack of your gaming adventures, making them even more thrilling and memorable.

140 - VINYL

Vinyl is like a disc that holds music inside, just waiting to be played. It's made of a special material that captures sound in grooves, like secret messages etched into a treasure map. When you place it on a record player or turntable and spin it around, a needle glides along the grooves, magically transforming them into music that fills the air. Vinyl records have a magical charm that invites listeners to dive into the rich sound of the past. Vinyl is one of the 'formats' you can get music on like cassettes, CDs, or digital streaming. Vinyl records are still popular today and many people love to collect them. When an older person says "I have that album", they usually mean they have it on vinyl because that format was probably the most popular when they grew up.

141 - VOCAL COACH

A vocal coach is like a seasoned chef who helps budding singers craft their voices as if they were perfecting a delicious recipe. They are like skilled gardeners nurturing plants, helping voices bloom and flourish like the sweetest fruits. Just as chefs teach new cooks the secrets of their favorite dishes, vocal coaches help singers find their vocal flavors and textures. With each lesson, a vocal coach can add a new layer of richness and depth to the singer's sound like a football coach will help you get better at playing football. Like someone helping you with your homework. A vocal coach guides singers on a journey of voice discovery, helping them create melodies as delightful as their favorite foods.

142 - XLR CABLE

Some singers have microphones (mics) with no cables or wires, called "wireless microphones". Some have a long wire called an XLR cable. They act like a sturdy link, connecting musical instruments and audio gear like microphones securely, similar to a strong rope that binds mountain climbers to their tools. An XLR Cable carries sound signals to where we can hear them. Used to join microphones, instruments, and other audio devices to mixers, amplifiers, and speakers, an XLR cable makes sure the sound gets there smoothly.

Whether you are in the studio, on stage, or during live performances, XLR cables play an important role in delivering clear and perfect audio (sound), ensuring every note, voice, and sound effect is heard clearly.

Look out for the Second Edition of 'Learning the Language of the Music Business', part of the 'FishFace NoodleHead' Series. Not Afraid to Ask and Never Afraid to Make Mistakes.